MUGGLE BORN

BECOMING THE MASTER MAGICIAN OF YOUR LIFE

I0167289

BOOK TWO

Michele Doucette, M. Ed.

MUGGLE BORN: BECOMING THE MASTER MAGICIAN OF YOUR LIFE: BOOK TWO

ISBN 978-1-935786-97-9

Printed in the United States of America by

St. Clair Publications

PO Box 726

McMinnville, TN   37111-0726

http://stclairpublications.com/

TABLE OF CONTENTS

What lies before us and what lies behind us are small matters compared to what lies within us; and when we bring what is within out into the world, miracles happen.
Henry David Thoreau

The path comes into existence only when we observe it.
Werner Heisenberg

At least ninety per cent of our mental life is subconscious, so that those who fail to make use of this mental power live within very narrow limits.
Charles F. Haanel

AUTHOR'S NOTE

As a writer, it is of the utmost importance to write about what you know, what you feel, what you believe, what you experience, for in doing so, the intended audience will be able to resonate with the deep passion put forth in the words on the page.

———— ✿ ————

Throughout this text, I have attempted *not to use* the word God, mainly because individuals hold to their own specific term within their individual belief system; instead, I have chosen to use the term Source (with a capital S) in reference to the many names that abound for the same.

THE PURPOSE BEHIND THIS BOOK

A good friend of mine asked me to share my purpose for the writing of this book.

MUGGLE BORN: BECOMING THE MASTER MAGICIAN OF YOUR LIFE: BOOK ONE

A magician is an individual that has been likened to a sorcerer, a wizard, a conjuror, a magus; someone whose wisdom, whose formidable skill, whose influence, whose art, seems to be magical.

In reference to the tarot, the Magician is the bridge between the world of the spirit (inner world, spiritual plane) and the world of humanity (outer world, physical plane) in that he/she takes the power of the universe and channels it through his/her own body and directs it, outward, to the physical plane.

As the Magician, you have the power and energy to create a new life cycle for yourself.

As the Magician, you have the ability to take the power of the universe and manifest your desires.

Knowing that you create with every breathe that you take, whether you believe this to be true or not, it is imperative that you learn to create from a conscious (awakened) and deliberate state of existence.

Enlightenment is nothing more than a significant life-changing shift in perspective.

As the Magician, you possess the ultimate level of control over your life and the events within. It is the Magician that takes responsibility for who he/she is and what he/she can do.

You are comprised of the very same energy that permeates the entirety of the universe; this is the energy, the power, the force, that you have available to you.

Becoming a Magician is about shaping your life consciously and with loving intent.

Controlling the power of your mind is all about living a life of liberation. It is a liberated state of mind, a compassionate attitude and a reverence for all life that serves to comprise the life of the Magician.

Here to live the best version of ourselves; so, too, are we also the Master.

Change on the outside (physical world) manifests when change on the inside (thoughts, emotions, actions, beliefs) has already begun to take place; this is what allows us to begin to live a more magical life.

As more strive to change, committed to living the best version of themselves, it is my belief that this change is reflected in the collective consciousness as well.

Courtesy of the reading of this first book, you will be able to glean the necessary tools to assist with understanding the world on a metaphysical plane.

MUGGLE BORN: BECOMING THE MASTER MAGICIAN OF YOUR LIFE: BOOK TWO

Buddhist scripture says that ...... *Our life is the creation of our mind.*

As the CREATOR of your life, you are the MASTER of your own reality.

Everyone thinks of changing the world, but no one thinks of changing himself. Tolstoy

If you want to awaken all of humanity, then awaken all of yourself. Truly the greatest gift you have to give is that of your own self-transformation. Lao Tzu

—— ༄ ——

Introspection (contemplation, reflection) is a lost art.

Introspection and reflection are all about getting to know yourself at the core.

While knowing yourself is the beginning of all wisdom, it is mastery of the self that becomes your TRUEST authentic power.

———

To live a fully intentional life, as a Master, all of the choices and decisions that you make must be aligned with the core of who you are.

In the words of Ralph Waldo Emerson ...... *The only person you are destined to become is the person you decide to be.*

It was Mahatma Ghandi who said ...... *Our greatness lies not so much in being able to remake the world as being able to remake ourselves.*

———

In essence, magic can be described as *changing reality in accordance to comply with your will, your love and your imagination*, [1] meaning that magic is all about using your intention to create something that you want, to create something that you desire.

The moment you accept, and acknowledge, that you are the creator of your reality, that you create everything in your life, the good, the bad, the ugly, you have embraced the ethical code of the Magician.

This is the moment wherein you welcome the fact that you are in a powerful position to change whatever it is that you do not like about your current life. Of course, so, too, does this mean that you must be willing to embrace change, otherwise life becomes stagnant, boring, dull.

---

[1] http://www.beliefnet.com/Wellness/Personal-Growth/How-to-Live-Magically-Every-Day.aspx

Courtesy of the reading of this second book, filled with both I AM statements, as well as I AM affirmations, that have significantly impacted my life, I trust that you will begin to see new opportunities, new possibilities, new potentialities for living a totally magical life.

———— ❧ ————

If you don't like something, change it. If you can't change it, change the way you think about it.

Mary Engelbreit

I AM

If we really want to observe ourselves, and find out what we are, we need to understand that *we are really beings of energy and vibration*, radiating our own unique energy signature outward into the vast expanse of the universe.

———— ✦ ————

We have all, at some point, walked into a room, met someone, for the first time, and felt an instant rapport, an instant connection, with that person. This happens when your energy vibration and their energy vibration are a match; when this happens, you resonate with, and complement, each other's frequency.

Likewise, we have all felt a danger, a discomfort, an instant dislike, upon meeting someone for the first time. This happens when your energy vibration and their energy vibration are not a match.

These experiences shows us that, despite the fact that energy is invisible to the naked eye ... it is real, it exists, it is there to assist us.

— ✦ —

Our energy field extends well beyond the physical body, interacting with our environment; like a radio antenna, tuned to our very own station; our energetic body then informs the rest of our being, feeding us all of the information that we are vibrationally attuned to.

— ✦ —

Put simply, our energy field is responsible for what we attract, both positive and negative.

For all the great work that we may do with our mental, emotional and physical states, if the changes are not reflected in the energy field, we will continue to keep attracting the same old patterns.

— ✦ —

When you spend time with someone who is operating on a high vibration you feel great.

Alternatively, when you spend time with someone who is operating on a low vibe, then you may feel drained, or tired, after you spend time with them.

———— ✾ ————

These two words – I AM – hold substantial power, given that they precede the subconscious beliefs you program yourself with; it is for this very reason that we need to take more care with the word(s) that follow, for you are literally instructing yourself to think, believe, and feel a certain way.

What are you saying *to* yourself?

What are you saying *about* yourself?

Pay attention, not only to your words, but also to your thoughts, for you are telling your subconscious mind [1] what to filter out and disable, and [2] what to let into your awareness.

In essence, you are commanding the Universe to form an outer reality which matches the declaration of what you have stated to be true, be that positive or be that negative.

I AM antisocial	I AM smart
I AM bossy	I AM creative
I AM impatient	I AM organized
I AM aggressive	I AM independent
I AM selfish	I AM positive
I AM sick and tired of ……	I AM observant

You are the only one who gets to decide on the word that comes next, after you have already declared I AM, so be sure to choose wisely.

You believe what you tell yourself. You have the power to easily define (empower or restrict) yourself with your words.

Instead of *I am incapable* of securing a job, shift the awareness to *I am more than capable* of securing a job.

I AM abundance	I AM acceptance	I AM action
I AM admirable	I AM adorable	I AM adventure
I AM affectionate	I AM agreeable	I AM agility
I AM allowing	I AM altruistic	I AM amazing
I AM ambition	I AM anticipation	I AM appreciation
I AM ardent	I AM attraction	I AM authentic
I AM awareness	I AM awesome	

I AM balance	I AM beautiful	I AM beauty
I AM beloved	I AM benevolent	I AM blessings
I AM bliss	I AM boldness	I AM boundless
I AM bravery	I AM brilliance	

I AM calm	I AM candor	I AM capable
I AM caring	I AM celebrated	I AM celebration
I AM centered	I AM certain	I AM challenge
I AM change	I AM charitable	I AM cheerfulness
I AM clarity	I AM comfort	I AM comfortable
I AM committed	I AM competence	I AM confident
I AM considerate	I AM consistency	I AM content
I AM cooperation	I AM courage	I AM creative
I AM creativity	I AM curiosity	

I AM daring	I AM decisive	I AM delighted
I AM determined	I AM devoted	I AM dignity
I AM disciplined	I AM drive	I AM divine

13

I AM eager	I AM educated	I AM effective
I AM efficiency	I AM elegance	I AM elevated
I AM empathy	I AM empowered	I AM enabled
I AM enchanted	I AM encouraged	I AM endurance
I AM energetic	I AM energy	I AM enjoyment
I AM enlightened	I AM enlivened	I AM enough
I AM enthusiasm	I AM equality	I AM eternal
I AM exaltation	I AM excellence	I AM excitement
I AM exemplary	I AM exhilarating	I AM expansive
I AM expressive	I AM exuberant	

I AM fabulous	I AM fair	I AM fairness
I AM faith	I AM family	I AM fantastic
I AM fascinated	I AM fascinating	I AM feasibility
I AM feeling good	I AM feisty	I AM festive
I AM fidelity	I AM fine	I AM flexible
I AM flexibility	I AM flow	I AM flourishing
I AM focus	I AM focused	I AM forgiving
I AM forgiveness	I AM free	I AM freedom
I AM friendly	I AM friendship	I AM fun
I AM future		

I AM generosity	I AM generous	I AM genial
I AM genius	I AM genuine	I AM giving
I AM glamour	I AM glory	I AM glowing
I AM God/dess	I AM goodness	I AM grace
I AM grateful	I AM gratitude	I AM groovy
I AM grounded	I AM growth	

I AM happiness	I AM happy	I AM harmonious
I AM harmony	I AM health	I AM healthy
I AM heartful	I AM helpful	I AM honest
I AM honesty	I AM honor	I AM hope
I AM hospitality	I AM humble	

I AM imagination	I AM improving	I AM incredible
I AM independent	I AM ineffable	I AM infinite
I AM influence	I AM ingenuity	I AM inner peace
I AM innovation	I AM insight	I AM inspiration
I AM inspired	I AM integrity	I AM intelligence
I AM intensity	I AM interesting	I AM intuitive
I AM inventive	I AM invigorated	I AM involvement

I AM jovial	I AM joy	I AM joyful
I AM joyous	I AM jubilant	I AM just

| I AM kind | I AM kindness | I AM knowledge |

I AM laughter	I AM learned	I AM learning
I AM liberty	I AM life	I AM lively
I AM logic	I AM longevity	I AM love
I AM loving	I AM loyal	I AM luxury

I AM magic	I AM magnificent	I AM majesty
I AM marvelous	I AM mastery	I AM meaning
I AM meaningful	I AM mind	I AM mindful
I AM mindfulness	I AM motivation	

| I AM nirvana | I AM noble | I AM nurturing |

I AM oneness	I AM open	I AM opportunity
I AM optimism	I AM order	I AM organization
I AM originality		

I AM passion	I AM passionate	I AM peace
I AM perceptive	I AM persistence	I AM playful
I AM pleased	I AM pleasing	I AM positivity
I AM power	I AM powerful	I AM proactive
I AM purpose	I AM purposeful	

I AM POSITIVE ACTIONS

I AM POSITIVE ATTITUDE

I AM POSITIVE BELIEFS

I AM POSITIVE CIRCUMSTANCES

I AM POSITIVE ENERGY

I AM POSITIVE EVENTS

I AM POSITIVE MIND

I AM POSITIVE THOUGHTS

I AM POSITIVE WORDS

I AM A POSSIBILITARIAN

I AM qualified	I AM quality	I AM quaint

I AM radiant	I AM rational	I AM readiness
I AM ready	I AM real	I AM recognition
I AM recognized	I AM rejuvenated	I AM relaxed
I AM reliable	I AM remarkable	I AM renewed
I AM repose	I AM resilient	I AM resourceful
I AM respect	I AM responsible	

I AM sacred	I AM secure	I AM selflessness
I AM serendipity	I AM service	I AM skilled
I AM sincere	I AM sincerity	I AM smart
I AM sparkle	I AM special	I AM spectacular
I AM stability	I AM steadfast	I AM still
I AM stillness	I AM studious	I AM stupendous
I AM sublime	I AM sunshine	I AM support
I AM supportive	I AM sweetness	I AM synergy

I AM tact	I AM teamwork	I AM tenacity
I AM thankful	I AM tolerance	I AM tranquil
I AM tranquility	I AM transformed	I AM triumph
I AM true	I AM trust	I AM truth

I AM unified	I AM unique	I AM unity
I AM uplifting		

I AM UNCONDITIONAL

I AM UNDERSTANDING

I AM valid	I AM validation	I AM valuable
I AM value	I AM veneration	I AM vibrant
I AM victorious	I AM victory	I AM virtue
I AM virtuous	I AM vitality	I AM vigor
I AM vim	I AM vulnerable	

I AM warm	I AM warmth	I AM wealth
I AM welcoming	I AM wellness	I AM whole
I AM willing	I AM willingness	I AM wisdom
I AM wise	I AM wonderful	I AM worthiness
I AM worth	I AM worthy	

I AM yesability	I AM young	I AM youthful

I AM zany	I AM zeal	I AM zealous
I AM zestful	I AM zing	I AM zippy

As you can see after reading through the positive word lists provided, the words I AM quickly serve to determine, affect and alter your physical experience.

It has also been shared, by many, that I AM is the name of God; unfortunately, the true meaning (power, essence, substance, significance) is what had been lost.

This means that the words I AM actually equate to your real nature, your real self, your real identity, your consciousness, your awareness, your Spirit, the Presence of Source in you.

Whatever you attach to the words -- I AM -- you become, meaning your formless awareness (I AM) conditions Itself into the image and likeness of your concept or ideal. The word goes out (I AM ----------) and returns to you in the form that you have ascribed to it, the form that you have given it.

You are Source.

You are the "I AM that I AM".

You are consciousness.

You are the creator.

The mission of the I AM is happiness, a life lived, a life of peace, a life of love, a life of caring for self and others.

This is the mystery, the great secret, known by the seers, prophets, and mystics throughout the ages.

As you can see, these two words, I AM, are the most powerful words that you can say.

PERSONAL AFFIRMATIONS

It was Ralph Waldo Emerson who wrote ...... *The only person you are destined to become is the person you decide to be.*

———— ❦ ————

In the words of Daniel Nielsen ...... *Your mission, should you choose to accept it, is simply to unlearn the ways of ego, embrace unconditional love, and with the heart of a child, return to loving others.*

———— ❦ ————

In the astute words of Albert Einstein ......*The world as we have created it is a process of our thinking. It cannot be changed without changing our thinking.*

———— ❦ ————

This particular segment of the book fast became my personal favorite; herein you will find personal affirmations that have been created with much inner contemplation.

May they serve to benefit you as much as they continue to benefit me.

It's better to walk alone, than with a crowd going in the wrong direction.
- Diane Grant

I AM UNIQUE

While we have the same needs and may act in similar ways, as individuated aspects of, we are as unique as our fingerprints; an energetic signature that belongs solely to us.

You are here to embrace your uniqueness, to celebrate your uniqueness, to live your uniqueness.

You see the world with your own perception; while there exists a separate path for everyone, all lead back to Source through different experiences of life.

Be not afraid of being labeled eccentric (as has also been the case of this particular author).

AFFIRMATION

I AM more than my body, more than my image, more than my thinking, more than my feelings, more than my roles, more than my creativity, more than my gifts, more than my strengths, more than my talents, more than my experiences, more than my community, more than my country, more than my culture, more than my race, more than my beliefs, more than my interests, more than my passions, more than my endowments. I AM ME. I AM MYSELF. I AM UNIQUE. I AM IRREPLACEABLE.

I AM IMPORTANT

In a culture that celebrates selflessness and sacrifice, we are often deemed unimportant, expendable, and nonessential, and yet our job is to *become who we are*.

The sages of old have always stated that this wisdom, just waiting to be re-discovered, resides deep within; some do it with study, some get a mentor, some have to go on a long journey to find it.

Each one of us has a special task and responsibility that only he or she can fulfill.

It is your job to find yourself, to your unique place; no one else can do it for you.

Everyone matters; surely it is enough to know that we touch (and perchance, inspire) the lives of other people simply by existing.

AFFIRMATION

I AM important, not because of, or despite, anything. With all my flaws and my facets, I AM important to me.

I AM STARDUST

While *I am stardust* might sound like the line in a poem, and it certainly was a line sung by Joni Mitchell, almost every element on Earth was formed at the heart of a star.

Every element in the Periodic Table, aside from hydrogen, is essentially stardust; hence the carbon, nitrogen and oxygen atoms, in my body, is made from elements forged by stars. [2]

Due to the fact that our bodies are made of remnants of stars and massive explosions in the galaxies, we are forever directly connected to this vast, majestic universe; so, too, are we interconnected to everything in the universe, including each other.

Is not this oneness amazing to behold?

---

[2] http://www.thegreatstory.org/Stardustbackground.pdf

AFFIRMATION

A traveler on a cosmic journey, I AM conscious of the cosmos within me. I AM a perfect union of stardust and spirit. I AM the energy of the stars. I possess star power. My fascination with the heavens has been turned inward, to be internalized as a fascination with who I am and from whence I have come. I AM one with the totality of all life. I AM here to live this oneness, a universal brotherhood and sisterhood; as I give, so shall I receive. I AM becoming an irresistible force to create peace and protect the planet. In the merging of stardust and spirit, the essence of who I AM, I possess creativity, magic and alchemy. The moment for clarity has arrived.

I AM STRENGTH

Strength is knowing what suffering feels like and learning to rise above it.

Strength is about believing in yourself so passionately that you are not afraid of facing the situation at hand.

Strength is about having the capacity to resolve challenges.

Strength is telling yourself that you are good enough, brave enough, and strong enough to overcome that obstacle.

Strength is about realizing that you are capable of whatever you set your mind to.

Strength is about persevering.

Strength is having the power and goal-oriented mindset to chase your dreams.

Strength is having hope where hope was once lost.

Strength is about holding onto faith even through the darkest of times.

Strength is about taking each experience, the good and the bad, and learning a valuable lesson from it.

Strength is about being able to accept the circumstances we cannot humanly change.

Strength is about the ability to find the beauty in *every aspect* of your life.

AFFIRMATION

I AM the strength of the universe. I AM resolved to being the best person that I can be. I AM resolved to doing the best that I can with the experiences that present themselves in my life.

Courage comes in many different shapes, sizes and forms. [3]

Spiritual courage means being open and available to the profound existential questions (why we are here, what is my life for, do I have a purpose), questions that can be quite frightening.

Spiritual courage means opening ourselves up to our own vulnerability and the mysteries of life; spiritual courage means letting go of the need to control everything.

In words that have been attributed to Christopher Columbus ...... *You can never cross the ocean unless you have the courage to lose the sight of the shore.*

---

[3] http://examples.yourdictionary.com/examples-of-courage.html

AFFIRMATION

I allow the courage of my heart to dissolve any fears I experience. I am a brave and valiant warrior. I face my challenges with boldness and determination. My dreams are much more important than any fears I might have. To be courageous also means doing what you think is right, learning to BE your own person, holding yourself accountable (what you think, what you say, how you act) and remaining true to yourself (what you think, what you believe, what you say, how you act); hence, I AM courage in action.

I AM LOVE

Spiritual love involves a sense of connection to an underlying unity that exists; it is a love for the world, a love for all people, even for those we do not like.

Spiritual love is a choice to be kind and compassionate based on an awareness that on a non-physical level we are so interconnected that whatever I do (individual level) affects you, affects the world (collective level).

Spiritual love involves a desire for the highest good of all.

Spiritual love says, *I might be distressed by you or your behavior on a personality level, but I know that spiritually, we are all one and I wish us no harm.* [4]

True spiritual love knows that [1] we are the Love we seek, [2] we are the Beloved, [3] we are the Act of Loving, devoid of expectations and attachments.

---

[4] http://www.huffingtonpost.com/judith-johnson/laws-of-spirit_b_1663620.html

AFFIRMATION

In a culture that thinks love can only to be a relational thing, we have forgotten the importance of BEING love (seeing, and embracing, the wonder, the joy, the beauty that abounds). I treat myself with kindness and respect. I honor the best parts of myself and share them with others. I give myself permission to shine and am proud of what I continue to accomplish. I look in the mirror and I love what I see. I love myself just the way I am. Knowing that I affect the world through my actions, demonstrating my unconditional love is the most important thing that I am here to do.

I AM PEACE

Although peace means something different to each person, each community, each nation, peace imbues all with a sense of well-being in all aspects of their lives.

Ultimately, peace is a state of mind reflected in our immediate environment; one that can only be achieved through using your unique skills and talents for the good of the whole as all of your own needs are met.

Inner peace (or peace of mind) refers to a state of being mentally and spiritually at peace, with enough knowledge and understanding to keep oneself strong in the face of discord or stress.

If there is light in the soul, there will be beauty in the person. If there is beauty in the person, there will be harmony in the house. If there is harmony in the house, there will be order in the nation. If there is order in the nation, there will be peace in the world.

-- Chinese Proverb

AFFIRMATION

What I cannot change, what I cannot influence, I must accept, I must release. Living in the present moment allows for stillness, and it is within this stillness that I AM able to find the peace that exists within. Peace of mind is simply a matter of where I place my attention. I AM at peace with myself and the world around me. I AM an instrument of peace. I AM centered in love, radiating peace out to the world around me. I surrender to the spacious presence of effortless being. My mind is still, my body is calm and I am at peace. I believe in a world where peace reigns supreme. I AM committed to a vow of non-violence in my speech, my thoughts and my actions.

———— ❦ ————

To be at peace is to create peace.

I AM COMPASSION

When we see someone in distress, feeling their pain as if it were our own, and striving to eliminate, or lessen, that pain, this is a demonstration of compassion; hence, qualities like sharing, readiness to give comfort, sympathy, concern and caring, all of these are outward manifestations of compassion. Compassion, then, can be seen as the ultimate embodiment of one's emotional maturity.

As an interesting side note, when you live your life as an instrument of compassion, your body produces more DHEA, the hormone that counteracts the aging process.

Compassion can also be illustrated as a form of non-action whereby you simply let matters take their determined course.

Compassion can further be illustrated as stepping back from your own mind; the display of a non-dualistic world where subject and object have ceased to exist.

AFFIRMATION

When I AM mindful of the fact that the actions I take are caring, loving and kind, I personify compassion. Every time I smile, I spread positive energy into the world. As I give to others, I receive in peace and happiness. As I come to better understand myself, I have a greater understanding of humanity.

———— ❧ ————

In the words of Albert Einstein ......*A human being is a part of the whole called by us universe, a part limited in time and space. He experiences himself, his thoughts and feeling as something separated from the rest, a kind of optical delusion of his consciousness. This delusion is a kind of prison for us, restricting us to our personal desires and to affection for a few persons nearest to us. Our task must be to free ourselves from this prison by widening our circle of compassion to embrace all living creatures and the whole of nature in its beauty.*

I AM UNDERSTANDING

To understand is to know that if you but take the time to see, to feel, to reflect, to meditate within, you will see that Source exists everywhere, *within all things and within all beings.*

To understand is to know that you need not seek anything outside of your Being, for all that you need resides within.

To understand is to know that you must allow others the time and opportunity to experience their own freedom, their own resolution, without judgment.

To understand is to know that when you respond to people with love and compassion, you readily move from conflict to harmony.

To understand is to remember that we are *continually evolving and changing* as per our own individual experience(s).

To understand is to know that living a life of gratitude, trust, love and peace is what generates more of the same.

To understand is know that we alone determine how, and to what degree, we progress along our evolutionary path, moving past our illusions of limitation to the freedom that lies beyond.

To understand is to know that we create the life opportunities of our choice.

To understand is to know that we determine and select which path(s) to take; it is to be remembered that the primary tool for this journey is naught but life itself.

To understand is to acknowledge that individual truths, as held by you, as held by me, are *all* true, for each expresses the truth(s) of the experience at any given moment in time.

To understand is to be willing to Become unlimited in your truth, remembering, always, that truth is ongoing, evolving, being created every moment by every thought you have.

To understand is to learn to Become multi-faceted in your truth means that you are not *one* truth, but *all* truths.

To understand is to become who and what you truly are by both knowing and accepting that Source *speaks through feelings*, for they will be your guide to truth, directing you onward toward your individual path of enlightenment.

To understand is to remember that the keys to compassion lie in your ability to embrace *all* experiences as part of the one, without judgment.

To understand is to demonstrate love through compassionate allowing, meaning that you must love others enough to *allow* them the range of their experience.

To understand is to live the truth that you *feel* inside.

To understand is to is to live life *consciously*.

To understand is to *live fully* and *with intent*.

To understand is to be *happy*, to be *joyful* and to be *filled with peace*.

To understand is to *know* that Source is not separate from you, to *know* that you and Source are one and the same.

To understand is to know that we are here to *live lives of unlimited love*, that we are here to *live lives of unlimited joy*.

To understand is to know that each path is a valid one, all leading to the same destination, all leading to their truest nature as guided by compassion.

To understand is to know that we are here to feel the feelings, engage the emotions, think the thoughts; for they are what allow us to experience ourselves in all ways.

To understand is to break the cycle of collective response, thereby becoming the higher choice.

To understand is to *transcend polarity while still living within the polarity* in an effort to move forward with life, a life filled with freedom, resolution and peace.

To understand is to demonstrate your Becoming; the healing of this world will come about as a result of the healing of thoughts, feelings and emotions.

To understand is to demonstrate the ability to express forgiveness, allowing others the outcome of *their* own experiences, without changing the nature of who you truly are, is the highest level of mastery to which you can attain, for therein lies the healing of all illusion, all separation, all duality.

AFFIRMATION

I AM empathic understanding.

Commissioned by Nick Bunick

author of *In God's Truth*

Reprinted with permission

I AM WEALTH

Wealth can be defined as [1] *an abundance of valuable possessions or money*, [2] *the state of being rich; material prosperity*, [3] *having plentiful supplies of a particular resource*, [4] *a plentiful supply of a particular desirable thing*, or [5] *one's well-being; prosperity*.

Emotional wealth = emotional fulfillment

Mental wealth = being rich in the knowledge of how to lead an emotionally satisfying and successful life

Physical wealth = the tangibles in our life (the things you can see, touch, feel, and move)

Spiritual wealth = striving for a simple life, a happy life, a life that is debt-free

AFFIRMATION

In the infinity of life where I am, aligned with the energy of abundance, all is perfect, whole and complete. My actions create constant prosperity. In my life, money and spirituality co-exist in harmony, expanding my life opportunities and experiences, creating a warm, positive, nurturing impact. Being wealthy gives me joy, happiness and peace of mind. I love knowing that I can help humanity with my wealth. I delight in the financial security that is a constant in my life. My wealth derives from honesty in everything I do. All my needs and desires are met, even before I ask. I make choices that are beneficial to me. I rejoice in the success of others, knowing there is plenty for us all. My good comes from everywhere and everyone. My heart is so very grateful for the wealth in my life. Money likes nothing better than to be plentiful in my life. I feel great joy in providing for my family and those I love. I am totally open and receptive to the abundant flow of prosperity that the universe offers.

I AM FORGIVENESS

Forgiveness does not mean that you deny the other person's responsibility for hurting you.

Forgiveness does not minimize, or justify, the wrong.

Forgiveness is a commitment to a process of change.

As you learn to let go of the negative emotions (anger, bitterness, confusion, resentment, vengefulness), moving away from your role as victim (and thereby releasing the control and power the offending person and situation once had on your life), you learn to embrace peace, hope, happiness, health, gratitude and joy in its stead.

Forgiveness also leads to [1] healthier relationships, [2] greater spiritual and psychological well-being, [3] less anxiety, stress and hostility, [4] lower blood pressure, [5] fewer symptoms of depression, [6] stronger immune system, [7] improved heart health and [8] higher self-esteem.

AFFIRMATION

The past is gone. I choose to live in the now, following the principle of live and let live. In following the path of forgiveness, life appears as a new, clean slate, a tabula rasa, if you will, wherein I can draw my new life plan as I wish. Each day is a new opportunity to evolve, to learn, to love. As Mahatma Ghandi once stated, *forgiveness is the attribute of the strong.* I AM that attribute.

I AM TRUTH

It was Winston Churchill who once stated ... *Men occasionally stumble over the truth, but most of them pick themselves up and hurry off as if nothing had happened.*

In relativism, all points of view are equally valid and all truth is relative to the individual.

As per Sartre's existentialism, we are not trapped by objectivity; rather, the lack of eternal, immutable truths allows us to create what is true for ourselves. [5]

I am free to choose my truths, and in doing so, I shape my own life, for without subjective truth, there can be no self-determination.

Truth is the nature of all souls; no individual has an exclusive claim on that which is deemed to be truth.

---

[5] https://philosophynow.org/issues/86/What_Is_Truth

While truth is difficult to define, we know that truth is [1] not error, [2] not self-contradictory, and [3] not deception (although it is true that while many individuals *act* in a deceptive manner, the act of their deception, in and of itself, is not truth).

AFFIRMATION

I am energized by truth and love. By living in the now, I acknowledge the presence of truth in my life. A student of my own soul, I continue to search for my deepest truth(s). Knowing that I am responsible for myself, I live my life, with integrity and compassion, in exuberance with these truths. I see the truth and beauty that is life, that is present in every atom, that is manifest in every being.

I AM HOPE

Hope is an emotional belief, an optimistic attitude of mind, a positive motivational state, based on an expectation of positive outcomes, events and circumstances.

Hope is not the same as having a positive attitude.

Hope is not the same as positive thinking (which can be denoted as a systematic process used in psychology for reversing pessimism).

Hope is the recognition, within the human heart, that something better is attainable.

AFFIRMATION

Life is a blessing. I look toward to my future with hope and happiness. Great opportunities come my way all the time. When I feel down, upset or afraid, I give myself a few moments to honor those feelings before reflecting upon what it is that I may be able to do to better the situation and/or what it is that I am meant to learn from the situation. In every circumstance, I strive to make the best of what I have, knowing that my future is bright.

I AM BEAUTY

The greatest beauty secret lies in our attitude towards life, for such is reflected in our face for all to see.

Our attitudes are reflections of our beliefs.

Our beliefs are created by the thoughts we continue to repeat throughout our lives.

In addition, we continue to broadcast our attitudes to the world via body language and facial expressions.

Over time, we begin to look exactly how we think and feel, meaning that all of the negative thoughts and feelings that you dwell upon are present for everyone to see.

Take a good look at yourself in the mirror; if you do not like what you see, adjust your thinking.

If you want to look beautiful, practice thinking beautiful thoughts; enjoy life, smile, laugh as much as you dare and be happy, for this is the secret to becoming beautiful.

AFFIRMATION

My face always wears a genuine smile that reflects the joy in my heart from knowing who I AM. Through my smile, people can feel the love that radiates from my soul. Others can see true beauty in me by the way I speak to them; hence, I choose my words carefully, making sure that I am respectful to those around me. My speech is filled with fairness and truth. I draw beauty from my self-confidence. I actively seek the beauty that exists in the ordinary and seemingly mundane. I AM beautiful just the way I AM.

I AM GRATITUDE

Feeling sincere gratitude for the good in your life is a powerful way to tap into positive energy, amplify it and allow it to flow more easily.

Having an attitude of gratitude allows you to focus your mind on the positive realities that already exist in your life; in doing so, not only do you magnify positivity within your mind, but you also attract more positive into your life.

You are genuinely grateful when your ego gets out of the way; as a result, the state of open receptivity, of surrender to Source, needs to exist before gratitude has any spiritual usefulness.

An attitude of gratitude has been linked to [1] better health, [2] sounder sleep, [3] less anxiety, [4] less depression, [5] greater satisfaction with life, and [6] kinder behavior towards others.

AFFIRMATION

My thoughts are focused on positivity and thankfulness. I take the time to be grateful for the simple things: a beautiful blue sky, the sound of laughter, a hug from a friend. My life is full of so many things to be grateful for; so, too, am I grateful for all the positive things that are yet to come my way. Thankfulness, appreciation and sincere gratitude are all important parts of who I AM. First and foremost, however, I am grateful for my very existence, knowing that I am here to heal, to grow, to learn, to love.

I AM CHANGE

Change is something that forces us out of our comfort zone, making it both terrifying and uncomfortable. We know that change is awkward, so learning to be flexible is paramount.

Without change, we become stuck in our ideas and philosophies; change, then, is necessary, because it keeps us moving.

Personal change is a reflection of our inner growth (through strength and endurance).

Personal change is a reflection of our empowerment.

In the words of John F. Kennedy ...... *Change is the law of life and those who look only to the past or present are certain to miss the future.*

AFFIRMATION

Change is absolute, positive and empowering. Change allows me to experience who I really am. Change continues to be a wonderful learning experience for me. Every day I am evolving into a more fulfilled person. Every day I am transforming myself into a more positive being. Every day I am attracting people who help me grow. I embrace change, adapting willingly and easily.

———⚮———

Michael Jackson MAN IN THE MIRROR Grammy Awards 1988 video [6]

A true genius, his knowledge, his wisdom, his insight, always transcended through to his astute and powerful lyrics. As the *man in the mirror*, we are all here to make that change, in ourselves, for the betterment of the collective whole.

_____

[6] https://www.youtube.com/watch?v=ljpl0neGk2Q

I AM HEART

To become heart, one has to live heart, one has to exude heart, one has to radiate heart; this means that I am here to create love, to create harmony, to create beauty, to assist in awakening the consciousness of humanity, to assist in awakening the divinity of each human being.

In this instance, heart does not mean the emotions (although it does include our emotions); instead, heart refers to the core of our being.

When you listen to the heart, when you are inspired by the heart, and have stepped back from your own mind, you are engaged in communication with Source.

Our spiritual heart knows the truth.

Our spiritual heart always directs us to Source (which also happens to be the source of our true self).

AFFIRMATION

The heart is found in stillness and is seen in action. As I demonstrate a life lived in love, harmony, beauty, acceptance, selflessness, compassion and authenticity, I become a beacon, a catalyst, an example for those who wish to do the same. The heart motivates, the heart transforms. Love is the answer to everything in life. I give and receive love effortlessly and unconditionally

ADDENDUM: It was during the writing of this book, that I was pleased to come across the I Am Heart Institute for Applied Meditation on the Heart. [7]

---

[7] https://iamheart.org/about_IAM/about_iam.php

I AM POSITIVITY

It was Mahatma Ghandi who stated ...... *A man is but the product of his thoughts; what he thinks, he becomes.*

Zig Ziglar writes that ...... *Positive thinking will let you do everything better than negative thinking will.*

Clearly, positive and negative thoughts can become self-fulfilling prophecies in that *what we expect can often come true.*

When it comes down to it, positive, optimistic people are happier and healthier, and enjoy more success than those who think negatively.

The key difference between those who think positively and those who think negatively is *how they think about and interpret the events in their life.*

AFFIRMATION

Positive energy flows through me; each cell of my being is awake and alive with joy. I radiate harmony, beauty, acceptance, selflessness, compassion and authenticity to everyone I meet. I release all negativity that is blocking the divine expression of who I AM by learning to trust the journey even when I do not understand it. It is my intent to see the positive side, the potential, and to make an continued effort.

I AM ACCEPTANCE

Every human being wants to be valued, to be needed, to be accepted, for who they are. A life without acceptance is often a life in which a most basic human need goes unfulfilled.

Acceptance liberates everything that resides within a person; when you are loved in that deep sense of complete and total acceptance, you become the unique and irreplaceable person that you are meant to be.

Acceptance also means that you are willing to let things unfold in a way that quite possible differs from what you originally had in mind.

AFFIRMATION

I accept responsibility for my attitude, my beliefs, my emotions, my thoughts, my words and my actions. I have the strength to accept what I perceive to be an obstacle; through acceptance comes freedom. I accept and enjoy all that is good and positive in my life. I am peace with who I AM and who I AM becoming. I choose to experience this moment, just as it is, taking full responsibility for making the most of my life. Through total acceptance, I allow myself to reach my highest potential. With love and acceptance, I easily change and grow.

I AM CREATIVITY

Creativity involves two processes ......

[1] thinking = the creative segment whereby you come up with ideas

[2] producing = the innovative segment whereby you bring those ideas to life.

If you have ideas, but do not act on them, it can be said that you are imaginative but not necessarily creative.

Relentless curiosity is what drives creativity.

Relentless curiosity is innate; the motivation to think does not come from others, but inside.

Relentless curiosity pertains to [1] the ability to ask questions on a constant basis, [2] the ability to question yourself, [3] the relentless pursuit of knowledge and truth (by learning to ask better questions), and [4] the ability to solve the most challenging problems by keeping an open mind.

Interestingly enough, the enlightened mind is one that relentlessly pushes the boundary of knowledge wherein you stretch yourself to look deeper, to listen harder, to interpret better, to connect the unconnected, all by way of maintaining an open mind.

AFFIRMATION

I exude infinite, creative energy. Being positive improves my creativity. I am highly receptive to the inspiration the universe sends my way, forever grateful for my imaginative mind. I love exploring new ideas, new possibilities, new potential. I embrace innovation.

I AM KNOWLEDGE

Knowledge is the accumulation of facts, data, ideas and skills that we acquire through study, research, investigation, observation or experience.

KNOWLEDGE = information, intellectual, known

The more you seek knowledge (meaning all knowledge), the more wisdom you will experience; knowledge, then, is but the doorway to wisdom.

Knowing that all knowledge that the world has ever received comes from the mind, that the infinite library of the universe has always resided within our own mind, when we *learn* something are we actually *re-discovering* something that has long been inherent, yet forgotten?

The attainment of knowledge, as you can see, may well be very much steeped in paradoxical understanding.

AFFIRMATION

As I relax into each situation in my life, I expand my knowledge and understanding. A permanent student of life, I seek to expand my mind. Forever keen to learn new things, I am always open to learning. My calm mind opens me to inner knowledge. My inner being is connected to the limitless wisdom of the universe. There is always something for me to learn in every situation. The knowledge that I am gaining empowers me to become the person I am meant to be; so, too, does it help me see that I am not here to change anyone other than myself (what I believe, what I think, how I respond).

I AM POWER

In the words of Barbara Geraci ...... *Our background and circumstances may have influenced who we are, but we are responsible for who we become.*

I have power over my mind; it becomes in the realization of this very fact that I find inner strength.

What I achieve inwardly always changes my physical reality, meaning that my inner thoughts manifest themselves through my actions, impacting the outer world (the physical world) around us.

Knowing that our individual actions affect the collective, meaning those around us, whether we choose to acknowledge this or not, each of us has a crucial role to play; therein lies the inherent responsibility of each individual.

It was Plutarch who believed, as do I, that happiness is the result of one's conscious effort in striving for a life of virtue.

AFFIRMATION

I AM the CEO of my life. I have the power to choose. I choose a more direct path to higher awareness. I choose to joyously leap out of my bed and greet my morning with a glad heart. As I inhale deeply, I choose to open up every cell in my body to all the positive vibrations of the universe. Negativity does not exist in my world. I am surrounded by positive vibrations. I choose to take care of myself, first and foremost, so that I can take care of others. I am the sum total of my choices which make me who I am. I celebrate what it is that makes me unique and irreplaceable.

I AM CONSCIOUSNESS

Consciousness refers to the state of being conscious; having an awareness of one's own existence.

Having an awareness of your existence means having an awareness about your surroundings, your thoughts, your emotions, your words, your actions.

In the words of Dr. Amit Goswami, Theoretical Nuclear Physicist, University of Oregon Institute of Theoretical Science ...... *If ordinary people really knew that consciousness, and not matter, is the link that connects us with each other and the world, then their views about war and peace, environmental pollution, social justice, religious values and all other human endeavors would change radically.*

There is also a higher consciousness that exists, one that is the universal power that sustains life.

Eugene P. Wigner, Nobel Prize winner and one of the leading physicists of the twentieth century shared ...... *It will remain remarkable, in whatever way our future concepts may develop, that the very study of the external world led to the scientific conclusion that the content of the consciousness is the ultimate universal reality.*

In words shared by Mooji ...... *Develop the habit of thinking of yourself as consciousness, not as the body or a person.*

AFFIRMATION

I create my life consciously and powerfully. I know in each moment I am free to choose. I know my attitude shifts my reality. I can react or I can respond. I know that I am responsible for everything that happens in my life. What drives my life is the energy that I generate in each moment. I choose to live consciously in every moment of my life, in awe of the abundance that nourishes my mind, body and soul. I continue to operate from a consciousness of love and abundance. I attract into my life what I AM.

I AM CONSCIOUS AWARENESS

Consciousness (cognizance, mindfulness, introspection, realization, recognition, reflection, sentience) leads to conscious awareness.

Conscious awareness involves [1] being mindful of your thoughts and intentions in all your actions, [2] knowing and being awake to what you may be unconscious of, and [3] pursuing to know thyself.

Learn to observe (and be a witness to) every act you engage in, every thought that passes your mind.

The more watchful you become, the less your internal chatter; your thoughts become more manageable and you gain a new clarity.

A clear mind is a happy mind.

As you grow in your awareness, your inner growth will explode because you begin to let the deepest parts of your being rise to the surface.

AFFIRMATION

The love of self is the gateway to all that is love. As I seek to make this transformational truth my personal reality, I am strengthened. The closer I listen, the more profound the truth becomes. I intend to live today from my purest intentions for the highest good of all.

———— ❧ ————

In truth, conscious awareness refers to one's awakening to a spiritual consciousness (as opposed to a material consciousness), journeying from the finite to the infinite, from the visible to the invisible.

Conscious awareness is key to spiritual transformation.

I AM MAGICAL

Perhaps my mission is to help you, the reader, come to the realization that magic is real, that magic exists within you.

Every thought you think, every feeling you emote, every word you speak, every action your perform, casts a spell of energy that flows into the universe, shaping your reality. In truth, we are all Muggle born; yes, just like the courageous Harry Potter.

For me, words are magic in that they have the power to inspire, to create, to instigate necessary change; so, too, is it the level of consciousness produced by the feelings, by the thoughts, by the words (mantra or affirmation) that create the change.

My chief motive for expressing myself with words (via books) is to *help spread the magic around* for all to experience.

Living a life of magic involves shaping your life from a mindful, lucid, awakened and conscious perspective, with loving intention, for yourself and for the greater good (the world).

Living the life of a magician also involves taking personal ownership and responsibility for every thought you think, every feeling you emote, every word you speak, every action your perform.

AFFIRMATION

Knowing that the reality of my life is a mirror of the words I speak and the thoughts I think, I wake up each day feeling inspired and excited. Life is all about magic, dreams, synchronicity, ebb and flow (going with the flow; the path of least resistance), creating by way of mind over matter, because thoughts are things. I embrace the magic of life that is fun, beautiful, warm and true.

I AM POWERFUL

Thoughts are powerful; they affect physical matter. [8] [9]

Knowing that they have a direct, measurable influence over the outside (physical) world, so, too, do they affect the inside (physical) world.

Your mindset matters.

The mind unleashed is a wonderful and powerful thing; so, too, can abusive words (and intentions) be used, as weapons, to hinder, to dis-empower, to destroy, so take time to choose them with care.

Replace harmful thoughts with positive thoughts for therein lies the alchemy behind using positive affirmations to change your life.

---

[8] http://www.spiritscienceandmetaphysics.com/proof-that-our-thoughts-effect-physical-matter/

[9] http://www.creatingconsciously.com/books/emotowaterbook.pdf

AFFIRMATION

I am the architect of my life; I build its foundation and choose its contents. I wake up each day with strength in my heart and clarity in my mind. My body is healthy. My mind is brilliant. My soul is tranquil. While I cannot control everything that happens to me, I *can* control the way I respond; my response (not my reaction) is my power. Happiness and laughter are my beverages of choice. I radiate grace, charm and exuberance.

———— ⁓ ————

Some ancient philosophical scriptures explain that the entire world, as we know it, was created by words. In Sanskrit, the term for this creative energy (that expresses itself through syllables and words to create the universe) was *Matrika Shakti*, the Mother Power.

Do you best to speak (and think) happy, uplifting and positive words so that you may find yourself living a more happy, uplifting and positive life.

I AM INSPIRATION

You inspire others by caring about them.

You inspire others by taking a stand for what you believe in, by setting an example.

You inspire others by being vulnerable, by being honest about who you are, by being upfront about your own struggles and difficulties.

You inspire by practicing integrity, always speaking the truth (even when it may be difficult to hear).

You inspire others by talking about the people who have inspired you, the books that have inspired you, the circumstances and situations that have attributed to your personal growth.

You inspire others by listening to them.

We all have the ability to inspire others whether we realize it or not.

When we inspire others, a connection is made; this inspiration brings about hope, energy and a path of possibilities.

It is my hope that, as an author, I am able to empower others to want to be an inspiration to others.

AFFIRMATION

I choose to let inspiration find me as often as possible. I exercise my imagination at every opportunity. I am ready to act on all inspiration that comes to me. Every day I read something positive, insightful and inspiring. I combine inspired thought with intelligent action, confidently following my instincts in all things. I inspire, and empower, others to their greatness. I love being an inspiration to others. Inspiration always arrives when I am fully focused in the moment.

I AM AUTHENTICITY

Affirming your true self means [1] taking action to meet your needs, [2] expressing who you really are, [3] thinking good thoughts about yourself and [4] taking action to do what you really want.

Neuroscience continues to substantiate the body-mind connection that exists; we know that [1] hormones (chemical messengers that are secreted directly into the blood), [2] neurotransmitters (brain chemicals that communicate information throughout our brain and body, relaying signals between nerve cells, called neurons) and [3] neuropeptides (small protein-like molecules (peptides) used by neurons to communicate with each other) all respond to emotion, imagery and thought.

Every time you affirm your true, authentic self, every cell in your body thanks you for the acknowledgment.

As E.E. Cummings has written ...... *It takes courage to grow up and become who you really are.*

Authenticity means being true to who you truly are and the reason you are here; being in alignment with your soul, an alignment that can only come from your actions, thoughts and behaviours.

In addition, the world needs us to show up and share our unique gifts.

AFFIRMATION

I am thriving as my authentic self. I am boldly powerful in my commitment to love who I am, where I am. Others are moved by my sense of self and through my example, they help themselves. Only through my personal internal alignment with integrity and honesty do I thrive. I AM who I AM.

I AM PASSION

What are your natural gifts? What are your skills and talents? What do you love to do? What is it that makes you feel most alive? What is it that you are passionate about? What is it that fills you with a sense of wonder? What brings you the greatest joy? When do you feel best about yourself? What are your personal strengths? What have others said that you are really good at? How do you most enjoy interacting with other people? How would you change the world, if you could?

When you start doing something that you love and time seems to stop, you have found your passion, you have found the path that you are meant to take.

In the words of Richard Leider ...... *The purpose of life is to live a life of purpose.*

You must always remember that your passion *is* your purpose. You are here to live your bliss.

AFFIRMATION

I live with passion and purpose. Passionate about my path, I pursue life with intensity and fervor. Dynamic and energetic, I AM passionate about what I do; what I do is who I AM. I AM passionate about writing. I am inspired to write. I AM smart, creative, curious and passionate; this fuels my thirst for knowledge. Steadfast in moving toward my dreams with determination, I AM committed to living my life passionately.

—— ✒ ——

In the words of Fabienne Fredrickson ...... *The things you are passionate about are not random; they are your calling.*

I AM AWAKE

In the words of Amma Bhagavan ...... *The root cause of all suffering is the sense of separate existence.*

An awakened human experiences no need for control. They become a witness to their thoughts; they become an observer of their body; they live in the reality of the present moment.

To say that one is awakening means they are *paying attention to the greater consciousness* (which is who you really are), no longer bound to the illusion of separate existence. Life is like a dream and you are the dreamer. According to author Timothy Freke ...... *Lucid living is recognizing that the person you appear to be, right now, is just a character in this dream of life. In reality you are the awareness which is dreaming the life-dream.* [10] [11] [12]

10

http://www.alternatives.org.uk/shared/files/upload/alternatives_frekearticle.pdf

In the astute words of Eoin Meegan ...... *While reading this I'm a part of your consciousness, you have created me, or pulled me in, for your own purposes, presumably to help you understand awakening. Therefore I only exist for you in this moment in your consciousness. But I also exist in my own right, in my world.* [13]

So, too, is it possible to become more lucid while you are awake. [14]

AFFIRMATION

More than my physical body, I AM a conscious adventurer in a world that is rapidly awakening and changing. I deeply desire to expand, to experience, to know, to understand; this is why I choose to live my life awake, embracing the totality of All That Is.

---

[11] http://www.hayhouse.com.au/lucid-living-waking-up-to-life
[12] http://www.gaiamtv.com/video/timothy-freke-lucid-living
[13] http://www.the-unscripted-self.com/whatisawakening.html
[14] http://www.spiritscienceandmetaphysics.com/lucid-living-3-ways-to-become-lucid-while-youre-awake/

I AM LIGHT

Pure light is a reference to Source, a reference the consciousness from whence we came.

OM is a sound that vibrates the oneness and harmony that exists within this shared consciousness.

OM embodies the essence of the entire universe, further deepened by the Indian philosophical belief that God first created sound and the universe arose from it.

As the most sacred sound, OM is the root of the universe and everything that exists and it continues to hold everything together.

Even though it is usually pronounced seamlessly so it rhymes with home (as I was initially doing), OM is made up of three syllables: A, U, and M, or, phonetically, *aaah*, *oooh*, and *mmm*.

[1] For *ahh*, relax the jaw. The sound rises from the belly, whereby the lips are parted, and the tongue does not touch the palate.

[2] In *oooh*, the lips gently come together as the sound moves from the abdomen into the heart.

[3] During mmm, the tongue floats to the roof of the mouth, and the lips come together to create a buzzing in the head; some say this syllable goes on twice as long as the others.

[4] Silence (the fourth syllable, if you will) follows while the sound fades into nothing.

Take the time to observe how you feel after having worked through these outlined steps.

The Aum symbol design can be seen as a symbolic representation of the various psychological compartments of the psyche; an inner dimensional map of the various compartments of human consciousness and the relationship each has to the divine within. [15]

When we take the time to chant OM together, we are aligning body, mind and spirit; we are aligning with each other; we are aligning with the universe because OM is the sound of the universe.

---

[15] http://www.religionfacts.com/symbols/aum

In addition, chanting OM also creates a link with those who have practiced before us.

I rather like the fact that this practice also serves to link me to the wisdom of the ancient sages, further inducing a profound sense of infinity (the lenses through which we see reality in its truest and more pure form).

AFFIRMATION

Fashioned of pure light and the dust of the Earth, my physical body is a container of light. I come from the Source and carry that goodness within me. Pure light flows through me and radiates out to bless all beings.

I AM SYNERGY

When something is synergistic, it means that the various constituent parts are working together to produce an enhanced result.

In the words of Ralph Walso Emerson ...... *There is one mind common to all individual men, and every man is an inlet to the same and all of the same.*

This quote addresses the concept of spiritual synergy.

Spiritual synergy encompasses seeing life through spiritual eyes with an emphasis on spiritual identity (empathy, love and appreciation of other souls) whilst also being committed to a united consciousness, a shared one mind consciousness.

In the words of Henry Ford ...... *Coming together is a beginning; keeping together is progress; working together is success.*

Embracing and living this synergism is what promotes a higher and a more vibrant energy, a more harmonious existence while all are here on the earth plane.

In the words of Wael Ghonim ...... *The power of the people is stronger than the people in power.*

AFFIRMATION

All the principles of heaven and earth reside within this physical body. My body, mind and spirit are aligned and working together, bringing much peace, joy, gratitude and success into my life. I choose to live our shared humanity, knowing that we belong together, knowing that our destinies are bound together, knowing that we can be free together, knowing that we can, in turn, create a glorious world together, living as members of one family; together, we are better, together, we are stronger.

I AM MAGNIFICENT

All are here to manifest their magnificence, offering their unique gifts to the world, because each of us has something special to offer in service to another.

Each of us can be likened to a canvas masterpiece, one that can only be completed with the brush strokes of our lives as we work toward claiming and expressing this magnificence.

In the words of Jacob Nordby ...... *Blessed are the bold and whimsical, for their imagination shatters ancient boundaries of fear for us all.*

The Egg by Andy Weir [16] [17]

The Egg: An adaptation of Any Weir's viral short story [18]

---

[16] https://www.youtube.com/watch?v=D1VN5zICGeU
[17] http://galactanet.com/oneoff/theegg.html
[18] https://www.youtube.com/watch?v=ehRggplMieM

AFFIRMATION

Every moment is an opportunity to make manifest our magnificence. I choose to see the light, the gift, the resplendence, that I AM to this world. I embrace the rhythm and the flow of my own heart. All that I need comes to me at the right time and place. I am deeply fulfilled with who I AM.

I AM PATIENCE

In the words of Saint Francis de Sales ...... *Have patience with all things, but first of all with yourself.*

Learning how to be patient, and staying calm under pressure, is something we all strive for.

Patience is not a genetic trait; it is not something that you inherit.

Patience is a skill, something that develops, over time, with persistent, and consistent, practice and effort.

Patience can become the honed (perfected) response to an undignified, and immediate, reaction (wherein one may do something, without thinking, or say something that cannot be retracted).

AFFIRMATION

Being patient is easy when I am focused in the present moment. While I AM learning that everything comes gradually, I also know that all great accomplishments require patience and persistence. I see having to wait as a perfect opportunity to be still and go within, to affirm and visualize my goals. It is my greatest desire to live each and every day with unlimited patience.

I AM WILLINGNESS

Willingness pertains to doing something out of choice and not because you have been coerced; when people are willing to do something, their minds are more open and receptive.

When something is done in willingness, there is no sense of resentment or hesitation.

Open-mindedness entails the willingness to explore themes (ideas, possibilities) that most people are not comfortable with, an important quality for spiritual seekers.

AFFIRMATION

I am willing to go beyond ego in order to reach out to that something more that exists, to liberate myself from the negative aspects (agenda) of the personality, to move from the head to the heart, to live in alignment with my beliefs that we are all interconnected, that what I do to another I do to myself. I consciously, willingly, deliberately extend love in every direction. Whilst giving up is easy and always an option, I choose to press on because I believe in my path. I am willing to work at what I love, no matter how difficult, how challenging, the job may be, no matter how exasperated I may become. I believe in my ability to change the world with the work that I do.

One of the key principles of quantum physics is that our thoughts determine reality.

As per the double slit experiment of the early 1900's, the determining factor of the behavior of energy (particles) at the quantum level is the *awareness of the observer* in that electrons under the same conditions would sometimes act like particles, and then at other times they would switch to acting like waves (formless energy), because it was completely dependent on what the observer expected was going to happen.

Can it not be said, then, that the quantum world is waiting for us to make a decision so that it knows how to behave?

In every sense of the word, we are truly masters of creation because *we decide what manifests out of the quantum field of infinite possibility* into physical form as we know it.

Given the energy of our thoughts, emotions, beliefs and intentions (the human energy field), we are influencing and informing the quantum reality within us, and around us, in every moment.

We know the force we call Source to be the energy and infinite consciousness behind creation; when we tap into ourselves as pure consciousness (through meditation), we experience an inseparableness from this same infinite creative consciousness.

AFFIRMATION

I create my world with the thoughts I think, with the emotions that I emote, with the feelings that I display, with the actions that I engage. Knowing this, I am consciously creating a better world for myself. I am the source of my own happiness. What I become is my choice, for only I AM the creator of my destiny, powerful beyond measure.

I AM ETERNAL

Eternal is synonymous with words like boundless, constant, enduring, everlasting, immortal, indestructible, infinite, never-ending, permanent, timeless, unceasing.

As individuated aspects of Source, each with the freedom, and will, to express ourselves, we are currently partaking of a physical experience, on this planet, as humans.

As shared by Pierre Teilhard de Chardin ...... *We are not human beings having a spiritual experience. We are spiritual beings having a human experience.*

On par with this human experience, we possess the capability to conceive, imagine and create. [19]

In the words of William Blake ...... *When the doors of perception are cleansed, man will see things as they truly are: infinite.*

___

[19] http://www.ebook.youreternalself.com/chapter1textlink.htm

AFFIRMATION

Deep at the centre of my being lies the infinite wisdom of the Universe. I accept that the Universal Force is unlimited; therefore I am unlimited. Every day I experience the universal magic of life, making my path a sacred one, thanking the Universe for all that I have. Everyone I meet is merely another form of this same Universal Force; by recognizing the divine in others, I acknowledge the divine in myself. I AM a beautiful being of light. I AM a magnificent spiritual being having a unique human experience. I AM a part of all things, eternal and infinite. As an instrument of the Universal Spirit, I AM an integral part of the Universal Force, as limitless as the Universe itself. I am forever empowered by the energy that I draw from the Universal Force. I AM an integral part of universal spirit.

I AM IMPECCABILITY

The first and most profound of don Miguel's Four Agreements is BE IMPECCABLE WITH YOUR WORD.

Whilst to be impeccable with your Word means to always use your Word in the direction of love and truth, it is not always as easy as it sounds here.

I was most impressed with the following explanation. [20]

Your word (small case) has to do with the things you say; these are phrases that you speak and write that come out as opinions, or comments, the thoughts in your head.

Your Word (upper case) has to do with the power you have to create through emotions, attitude, actions, what you refrain from, and what you express as your belief.

---

[20] http://www.toltecspirit.com/four-agreements/impeccable-word/

AFFIRMATION

Everything I say and do is for the higher good of all concerned. Always endeavoring to do the right thing, I accept total responsibility for my actions and am committed to living my life responsibly. I dare to uphold the truth, doing what I know in my heart to be the right thing. I live my life the way I would like to be remembered, demonstrating respect and treating others as I would like to be treated. Sincerity is a value that I honor every day. Speaking the truth is the only way I know. I strive to provide a positive example to all that I meet on my daily journey.

I AM INTEGRITY

Walking your talk is the path to personal integrity. Not only do you have to say what you mean, you also have to mean what you say, to demonstrate the same by way of action.

When we operate from a place of integrity, we speak from a place of wholeness; our words match our actions. In this instance, you will find yourself to be a much happier person.

As your word becomes more and more powerful, as you continue to speak from a place of integrity, your reality will begin to reflect that.

AFFIRMATION

I accept the great responsibility of true freedom, no longer caught up in the tolerance for careless, destructive and disempowering language. I am always open, honest and forward with my words and actions. I strive not to take anything personally so that I have more time to respond, from a place of empathy, love and understanding, thereby giving me less time to react, from a place that I no longer wish to visit. I am, at all times, personally accountable for my words and actions.

I AM CHOICE

You always have a choice in what you think, say and you do. While you may have little control over a situation that seems daunting and overwhelming, and you feel a sense of complete helplessness, you still have a choice as to how you respond in that situation. You can either continue to suffer in the face of the situation, making yourself out to be the victim, or you can muster your courage to take action, thereby becoming the victor.

If you keep thinking you have no choice over your situation, you will always remain powerless; the moment you take ownership for what is going on in your life, well, that is the very moment that an important and integral shift has taken place. Rather than feeling victimized by your situation, you begin gain power over it, one step at a time.

It was Voltaire who wrote ...... *The most important decision we make is to be in a good mood.*

AFFIRMATION

There is *always* a choice to be made. As I choose my thoughts, my words, my actions, I choose my life. Each day I choose to see things from the most optimistic perspective. I accept the decisions of others, and realize that it is their right to make their own choices. I choose friends who are positive and supportive. I consciously choose to nourish my mind with positive, uplifting thoughts. I choose to appreciate everything life brings me. I choose to be cheerful regardless of circumstances that arise. I choose to be healthy. I choose to do those things that I know will improve my life. I choose to experience life calmly and peacefully. I choose to feel good about myself. I choose to laugh at the outrageous things in my life. I choose to let go of any attachment to the past. I trust my inner voice to guide all my actions and decisions. I choose to greet the each day with a open and loving heart. In paraphrasing Ralph Waldo Emerson, *the only person I am destined to become is the person I decide to be.*

I AM ONENESS

Oneness means just one.

The concept of oneness involves discarding all ideas of separation from anything, from anyone.

Oneness means allowing yourself to simply be.

The closer you get to experiencing your original nature, the more peace, passion and purpose flows through you.

AFFIRMATION

I am connected to the totality all of life. I AM one Mother Earth. I AM one with this physical body. I AM one with the Universe. I AM one with all life. What is true of me is true of everyone; we are all learning to look within ourselves to find the wisdom to live harmoniously. I am helping to create a world where it is safe for all of us to love each other, without fear of reprisal or retribution.

I AM LIMITLESS POTENTIALITY

It is imperative that you, the reader, recognize that you are both Source and unlimited potential. You do not experience Source; instead, Source experiences itself through you. Quite simply, you are All That Is.

Source creates, actualizes and/or experiences from an unlimited potential perspective; a potential that is void of distinctions or boundaries, and therefore, has no limitations.

The moment you let go of your sense of being separate, awareness from an expanded perspective allows for that potential to express itself more readily through you.

We are much more than our problems.

We are much more than anything we are choosing or not choosing to experience in any moment or over time.

In the words of Anatole France ...... *To accomplish great things we must not only dream but also act, must not only plan, but also believe.*

AFFIRMATION

I live in a world full of possibility and potential. I have the power to change my life for the better. I have within me the potential to create my dreams and aspirations. I know that I am meant to do great things and I know that the Universe intends great things for me. I choose to think big. I feel so incredibly empowered about who I AM and what I AM becoming. I know that there are no limitations to life, save those created by my thoughts. I recognize and encourage the potential of others. I see people as they can be, and encourage them in this direction. I strive to realize the seemingly impossible. The potential of my mind is unlimited. There are no limits to what I can achieve in my life. There are no limits to who I can become. Today I let my wildest dreams take flight. Unlimited potential awaits my conscious acceptance.

I AM DETACHMENT

This incarnation is about you; do not focus on what it is that another soul is here to do, to learn, to grow from; rather, the emphasis needs to be placed on none other than yourself.

In the words of Ali ibn abi Talib ...... *Detachment is not that you should own nothing, but that nothing should own you.*

AFFIRMATION

I consciously commit to flexibility and detachment. I accept myself for who I am without judgment or criticism. I embrace detachment by choosing to be free from the opinions of others. I will no longer give my power away to those who try to control and manipulate me. I own my power and take responsibility for the choices and decisions I make each day. I give myself permission *not* to take anything personally, thereby moving one step forward to emotional detachment. I am able to let go of what no longer serves me. I am completely self-determined, displaying the freedom to live as I choose, whilst harming none, and fully accord others the same right.

I AM MYSELF

Whilst we are, indeed, individuated aspects of the same Source, I continue to experience life as naught but myself; so, too, do I appreciate the unique differences that abound, displayed by the other individuated aspects of this same oneness.

We all complement each other, making a complete whole, and yet what you have, no one else has, so take pride in your uniqueness.

Never doubt that ability that you possess to realize your true potential.

You have the right to be you.

AFFIRMATION

I respect myself. I honor the essence of who I am, allowing my light to shine brightly for all to see. I honor the wisdom of my soul and am consciously aware of the choices I make. I honor the wisdom of my soul and trust in the guidance that I receive. I release all negative thoughts and will only focus on the positive in my life so that I can continue to be an inspiration to those around me. I am able to see each day as a new opportunity to make things better. I AM my own oracle in that I AM able to delve within find the answers, that are needed. My success in life stems from my being happy with who I AM and who I AM striving to become.

I AM SPIRITUALITY

If we take our spirituality seriously, we must come to the realization that each of us are individuated aspects of Source (individual sparks of the same). Just as the whole is related to its constituent parts (Source is connected to us), so, too, are the parts related to the whole (we are connected to Source). It is your response ...... to the lack of connection that we feel with our own selves (body, mind and spirit) and the lack of connection we feel with one another ...... that matters.

As Chief Seattle has shared ...... *Humankind has not woven the web of life. Whatever we do to the web, we do to ourselves. All things are bound together, all things connect.*

By changing your perspective, you are able to change your experience.; in retrospect, therein lies the solution to the problem.

In the words of Ram Dass ...... *The quieter you become, the more you can hear.*

AFFIRMATION

I AM centered and calm, knowing there is a Presence within me, always guiding me to right action wherein love and compassion are the highest forms of intelligence. I AM fully present in everything I do. I AM unconditioned, formless, eternal consciousness. I embrace silence as the source of all deep understanding and wisdom. I AM still, alert and open to what is, for it is this inspiration and awareness that guides me in everything that I do. I embrace the personal and spiritual growth that is necessary for the evolution of Source. I AM anchored in the present moment. I am living my life in harmony with Source, allowing divine intentions to work through me as they manifest into the material world. I AM committed to the transformation of my consciousness. I AM living my life according to my highest vision that is inspired by love and joy.

I AM PROSPERITY

Most people immediately associate the term prosperity with monetary wealth.

Real prosperity, however, is an *inside* job, meaning that prosperity really comes from within.

You do not have to have a bank account overflowing with money to feel prosperous; doing things that [1] make you feel satisfied, [2] make you feel connected, [3] allow you to feel, and demonstrate, gratitude, [4] allow you to contribute to the happiness and well-being of another person ...... these are the type of things that enable you to *feel prosperous.*

Renewing your mind, changing your attitude, having a good relationship with people, performing random acts of kindness (as in the Pay It Forward idea), experiencing success; all of these can contribute to feeling prosperous.

AFFIRMATION

I prosper in everything that I do. My life is full of love and joy and all the material things that I need; the universe takes good care of me. I live in a state of complete fulfillment. Forever conscious of my true wealth, I give of my talents freely. An eternal being, my affluent prosperity is limitless. I allow the universe to bless me in surprising and joyful ways. My heart is so very grateful for the continued prosperity in my life.

I AM THE MOMENT

To live in the moment means being present, conscious and aware of the present with all of your senses.

Focusing on one thing at a time (the task you are engaged in, an object you are looking at, the food you are eating, the rhythmic flow of your breath) brings you back to the moment; when you live in the moment, you are truly living your life.

Refrain from multi-tasking.

Take the time to disconnect.

Take the time to meditate, to embrace the stillness within.

In the words of H. G. Wells ...... *We must not allow the clock and the calendar to blind us to the fact that each moment of life is a miracle and a mystery.*

AFFIRMATION

Each time I inhale blessings, I exhale gratitude. The now is where attention and intention intersect. All my power exists in the present moment. Being totally present in every moment opens my eyes to inspiring, new experiences. Each moment contains clarity and truth that can revitalize my life. I am fully awake and alive in each and every magical moment of my life. Each moment in my life is a new beginning. Each moment of my life is full of choices. I feel the joy of simply being present in every moment of my life. I see life as the greatest adventure, and NOW as the only time that counts. Inspiration visits me when I am focused in the present moment. Life is a series of moments, and I am fully present in each one. Time expands when I am in the Zone, doing what I love. Today I bless my life with infinite moments of being.

I AM CONTEMPLATION

Contemplation means to think profoundly (and at length) about something, to reflect on something, to deliberate over something, to ponder something.

Take the time to deliberate over your thoughts, your words, your actions, before responding.

As shared by Hafiz ...... *The words you speak become the house you live in.*

Take the time to meditate, to practice contemplation and tranquility.

In the words of Lao Tzu ...... *To the mind that is still, the whole universe surrenders.*

It was Alan Watts who said ...... *Meditation is the discovery that the point of life is always arrived at in the immediate moment.*

AFFIRMATION

As I relax in my mind, I relax in my body. By being still and quiet, I discover my inner wisdom. By quieting my mind, I allow answers to arise from within. Every moment I spend in quiet contemplation brings welcomed balance into my life. I emerge from meditation with renewed energy and inspiration. I play many roles in life, but the most important one is when I play none. I rejuvenate my being in the peacefulness of my inner sanctuary. My quiet mind is a peaceful sanctuary that I can visit any time. When my mind and body are still, my spirit reunites with the universal force that is all things.

I AM BALANCE

How does one learn to balance the extremes of functioning in society (survival, the logical mind) whilst also pursing spiritual enlightenment (happiness, the soul)?

In accordance with Adyashanti ...... *Enlightenment is a destructive process. It has nothing to do with becoming better or being happier. Enlightenment is the crumbling away of untruth. It's seeing through the facade of pretence. It's the complete eradication of everything we imagined to be true.*

Take the time to live a wholesome, functional life. Work hard and be rational, remaining focused and goal oriented, without getting too immersed in the materialistic world. Learn to maintain a reflective, metaphysical mindset, knowing, and embracing, that higher dimensions exist; this will surround you with a deep sense of peacefulness and inner joy so that you may begin to balance material demands with spiritual needs.

AFFIRMATION

Every day I achieve greater balance between my thoughts and my actions. I am creating a harmonious life, the perfect balance of femininity and intelligence. I balance my intellect with my heart, and receive peace, strength and wisdom in return. My day is a perfect equilibrium of reflection, recreation and resolute purpose. My immense power and quiet calm support each other perfectly. My physical, mental, emotional and spiritual selves are all in perfect alignment. My steadfast values lead me to live a life of harmony and balance. My vision keeps me focused and ensures equilibrium in my life. My work and home life are in perfect harmony. There is balance and order in my life at all times.

I AM FORTITUDE

Fortitude is about strength of mind, a steadfastness of mind, a moral strength, if you will, that does not waver, all in the pursuit of what is good.

Fortitude is what allows us to withstand the adversities in life with courage.

It is fortitude that grants one the resilience to resist and overcome opposition, thereby outlasting others; think, in this case, how important fortitude is in order to withstand peer pressure.

In the words of Francis Bacon, SR ...... *Fortitude is the marshal of thought, the armor of the will, and the fort of reason.*

Embrace spirituality, meditate regularly to develop mental clarity, take care of your physical body, cut off negative (draining) connections to people and circumstances that prevent you from realizing your true potential. Do not fear failure, solitude or struggle.

AFFIRMATION

The more successful I am, the more the world will benefit. I bring higher energy into the world through my acts of compassion and kindness. I fill my heart with compassion so that I can be of better service to others. I give to others openly and gratefully. Everything I give to others is a gift to myself. As I give, so, too, do I receive. With every smile, I am spreading positive energy into the world. I am committed to improving my corner of the world. I am sensitive to the needs of others. I love the feeling of helping people help themselves. I make a genuine effort to help people feel appreciated. I offer my assistance (time, skills, passions, wisdom, knowledge, monetary, emotional, spiritual) whenever I can. I only speak kind words about others, showing courtesy to everyone I meet.

I AM GRACE

When you speak your truth (what you know), Grace is standing beside you.

When you reach out and genuinely touch the heart of another, both of you are surrounded by Grace.

When you look at the events of your world with compassion and deep understanding, Grace is looking with you.

When you respond to a need greater than your own, Grace speaks through you.

In essence, Grace represents the presence of Source in the world; even more important, Grace represents the evidence of the greater personal relationship that you have with Source.

In the words of John Osborne ...... *Laughter is the nearest we ever get, or should get, to sainthood. It is the state of grace that saves most of us from contempt.*

AFFIRMATION

I am exactly where I should be. Free to choose the life of my dreams, my worth is not determined by my mood or my thoughts. Knowing that I am a sage in training, I celebrate the wisdom gained from making mistakes. With an awareness of the precious present, if I know better, I do better. I am the awareness of generosity flowing forth to everyone and everything. As we move toward our dreams, we move toward our divinity. Creativity is the natural order of life. Life is pure, creative energy. Energy is connection between past and future, between point A and point B, between you and me. In solitude, I remember my connection to others. Whilst I do not expect to find the light in all situations, I choose to radiate the light, to live my life as an example to others.

I AM WISDOM

Wisdom is the ability to discern and judge which aspects of knowledge are true, right, lasting and applicable to your life; so, too, is wisdom the ability to make sensible decisions and give good advice because of the experience and knowledge that you have.

WISDOM = the understanding and application of knowledge

Wisdom is something that is recognized by virtue of feeling (a warm sense of illumination, if you will). Wisdom does not need digesting, deliberating, debating or dissecting by doubt or reason; it breathes within you as calm surety and perfect peace, for it is then that you recognize, intellectually, that this knowledge has always been with you, just waiting for you to find it. [21]

---

[21]
http://www.controverscial.com/Knowledge%20vs%20Wisdom.htm

AFFIRMATION

Source gives me the discernment to make sound decisions. I trust myself to deal with each new development, with wisdom and grace, as it arises. I am magnetic, gentle and wise. I trust my inner wisdom. My wisdom gives me the ability to perceive, believe and proceed. Source gives me knowledge and understanding so that I can gain wisdom through my experiences. There are two key words of wisdom: pay attention.

―― ❧ ――

In truth, the essence of wisdom is emancipation from the tyranny of the here and now. [22]

22

http://www.personal.kent.edu/~rmuhamma/Philosophy/RBwritings/knowlegANDwis.htm

I AM VITALITY

Vitality refers to endurance, exuberance, stamina, spunk, physical strength and mental vigor.

As you work to transform your attitudes about life, changing your perspective (as needed), focusing on increased positivity, seeking love everywhere, delighting in the connectedness whilst living in the *authentic now* and accepting your true self ...... you will be able to discover personal meaning in your life, thereby achieving the balance that is both needed and necessary.

In the words of Ralph Waldo Emerson ...... *The first wealth is health*.

AFFIRMATION

My body is a reflection of perfect health. My body knows what it requires for optimum health. The cells of my body are vibrant and healthy. My chakras are aligned in perfect harmony with Source. My choices are intelligent and life-enhancing. The genetic coding of my body is constantly returning to its original perfect state. The more I relax, the healthier I become. Universal energy flows through every cell in my body. Universal spirit is in every atom of my being, and with my gratitude, restores me to well-being. With every breath I take, I am bringing more and more well-being into my life. As I wake up each and every morning, I am refreshed and renewed. A complete sense of well-being infuses my life. All of my thoughts are healthy thoughts. All the cells in my body are returning to their perfect original blueprint. All the cells in my body resonate in perfect harmony. An aura of perfect well-being surrounds my body and mind. As I take control of my mind, I also take control of my body. Breathing deeply elevates my mood and energizes my body.

I AM EMPOWERMENT

Spiritual empowerment entails an awareness of WHO and WHAT we are.

I know that I am an individuated expression of Source.

I know that Source permeates all life in the universe.

I know that by continuing to refine my perception(s) and opening my mind, the authentic self becomes more noticeable and life takes on greater meaning.

I know that as I continue to discover the Divine in everyone, as well as the good in all, my experience of everyday life shifts to a more harmonious perspective.

I continue to take responsibility for what is happening in and around my life, making all pertinent changes that bring me closer to a spiritual way of life and living.

We begin to see life, and others, from a wider perspective, an unbiased lens.

Through this spiritual receptivity, knowledge and consciousness, we awaken to the one-for-all and the all-for-one power that exists; have to get my Musketeer theme in here!

I am able to recognize the infinite qualities of good within everyone.

I am able to realize that I have, within me, infinite possibilities and unlimited potential.

I realize that every emotion is the result of either positive or negative thinking and that it is only through awareness of, and creatively working with, my thoughts, feelings and emotions that I am able to manifest more positive qualities within.

As I continue to grow increasingly aware of my actions and reactions, I become more spiritually responsible, able to grow into more a centred and loving individual.

If we truly wish to develop and manifest all that is good within us, we must endeavour to harmonise our lives with Source.

All life is sacred and ultimately derives its existence from Source; therefore, we should seek to become one with this sacredness that exists in everything and everyone, and respect and care for all life, including ourselves.

AFFIRMATION

I joyously leap out of my bed and greet each morning with a thankful and gracious heart. As I inhale deeply, I open up every cell in my body to all the good vibrations of the universe. I love myself and accept myself as I am. I am beautiful, healthy, prosperous and happy. I am well respected and appreciated. I am assertive and, at the same time, most considerate towards others. I am a compassionate, kind and caring person. No matter what obstacles come across my path, I overcome them with renewed inner strength. My inner strength is a mighty fortress. I find myself growing in wisdom, courage and good health, always responding to others with empathy, understanding and compassion. I am the sum total of my life choices. I celebrate what it is that makes me unique and unrepeatable. I get my work done effortlessly. I meet challenges bravely. Negativity does not exist in my world. I am surrounded by positive vibrations.

I AM CONFIDENCE

Spiritual confidence can be referred to as a palpable sense of absolute conviction, an absolute surety, a knowing that you know without knowing how you know (cognizance), an unshakeable sense of rightness.

In choosing consciousness, in choosing responsibility, in choosing assertiveness, in choosing purposefulness, in choosing integrity, in choosing authenticity ...... I am choosing to get to know who I am.

When I *know* who I am ...... I have discovered that I am none other than you.

The Eastern traditions say that doubt is one of the biggest obstacles to the profound discovery of enlightened awareness.

I choose not to doubt, but to trust in that palpable sense of absolute conviction, that absolute surety, that knowing that you know without knowing how you know (cognizance), that unshakeable sense of rightness.

AFFIRMATION

I believe in myself and my abilities. I always express my thoughts and opinions with confidence. I make sound decisions. I am not a victim of my circumstances. I have the ability to grow and change. Every moment is a gift. I love that I am unique. My confidence commands respect and attention. Confidence empowers me to take action and live life to the fullest. Feeling confident, assured and strong is part of my daily life. I have the knowledge to succeed. I always attract only the best of circumstances and the best positive people in my life. I am a vessel of happiness.

I AM EMPATHY

Empathy is the rare event where one person actually feels the emotions, problems and perspective of another person. Empathy is all about establishing a rapport and openness between people.

The best way to build empathy is to help the other person feel that they are understood; that means being an active listener.

In the words of Meryl Streep ....*The great gift of human beings is that we have the power of empathy.*

In the words of Joan Silk ...... *Human altruism is thought to be based, in part, on empathy. To be empathetic, you need to understand the thoughts and desires of others.*

As astutely stated by Barbara Kingsolver ...... *Empathy is the capacity to understand that every war is both won and lost; that someone else's pain is as meaningful as your own.*

AFFIRMATION

I am good at understanding the feelings of others. I am able to see situations from the vantage point of those around me. I am well known for my caring personality. People come to me for help in stressful situations. I enjoy helping others. I am able to see the good in everyone. Empathy comes naturally to me.

I AM INSIGHT

Insight is the deepest level of *knowing* and the most meaningful to your life.

Insight involves grasping the underlying nature of knowledge and the essence of wisdom.

Insight is a true understanding of your life (the microcosm) and the bigger picture of how everything is intertwined (the macrocosm).

INSIGHT = the awareness of the underlying essence of a truth

Insight can also be referred to as the second sight in keeping with those who *have eyes to see but do not see, and ears to hear but do not hear* (Ezekiel 12:2). In this case, the most important kind of seeing is the seeing of spiritual realities.

AFFIRMATION

I receive guidance and insight through meditation. I am able to see how things ARE, not as they APPEAR to be. Every day I read something insightful and inspiring. I accept my inner voice with reverence and respect. I combine inspired thought with intelligent action. I listen intently to the whispers of my soul. I spend my money on things that inspire and empower me. My inner being expresses itself through intuition and inspiration. My inner knowing is more powerful than belief. My inner sage guides me perfectly. My mind and the universal mind are one, therefore, my intuition is perfect. Whenever I ask for guidance, my inner knowing answers.

—— ❧ ——

Please take the time to visit The Insight Project. [23]

---

[23] http://www.trans4mind.com/spiritual/

PUTTING THE TITLE TO WORK

It has been a most liberating and exhilarating experience to write this book; even after over twenty years on the spiritual path, there is still much that I am continuing to learn, to experience, to resolve and grow from.

Each of us is an internal quest of re-discovery, of remembering who they are, of understanding the importance of merging heart and ego in order to live a life of wholeness, a life of love and compassion, a life of authenticity, a life of eternal awareness, a life of realization that ALL IS ONE.

As per the motto of the Royal Society of London ... *Nullius in Verba* ... take no one's word ... for what it is that you are here to uncover for yourself.

In the words of Carl Gustav Jung ...... *The privilege of a lifetime is to become who you truly are.*

You are strength, you are beauty, you are wisdom. Dare to believe in yourself. Dare to dream and live your life as if there were no limits to what you could do, be and have.

In these most astute words attributed to Jalāl ad-Dīn Muhammad Rūmī, simply known to us as Rumi ...... *You were born with potential. You were born with goodness and trust. You were born with ideals and dreams. You were born with greatness. You were born with wings. You are not meant for crawling, so don't. You have wings. Learn to use them and fly.*

You have your own path to walk, your own purpose to fulfill, your own passion to embrace.

In continuation, the words of Dhammapada are equally as powerful ...... *You are the source of all purity and impurity. No one purifies another. Never neglect your work for another's, however great his need. Your work is to discover your work and then with all your heart to give yourself to it.*

In that same light, I hasten to add the following ......

I implore you, the reader, to believe nothing simply because I, or anyone else, deem it to be true.

I implore you, the reader, to take the time to explore, to take the time to examine, to take the time to discern, that which resonates as truth for you, for therein you shall find the answers that you seek, the answers that shall set you free.

In continuation of the same, it is not enough to read my words, to reflect on them, to decipher what they mean, so, too, must you also be willing to apply the knowledge, the wisdom, the insight, that has been gleaned in order to affect the inner change that is needed.

WHY DO I WRITE?

I write for myself so that I may express, reflect upon and share my lived experiences with others, doing my best to show others what is possible.

I write for the pleasure and enjoyment.

I write for myself as much as I write for the individual.

I write for people who recognize that they, too, can do something for themselves, that they can work to improve their lives, their consciousness, their power.

I write for the people who are open minded enough to consider (to contemplate, to foresee) something new, something better, something liberating for themselves.

I write for people who have finally come to the realization that everything they seek, the answers and solutions to their own lives, comes from within, even if they know naught how to begin accessing that information.

I write for people who are ready to consider ideas, concepts, hypotheses, possibilities and probabilities that take them outside the parameters of their former conventional lives.

I write for the people who see life as a wonderful gift through which they can express themselves, their talents, their gifts, their passions, so that all may enjoy.

So, too, is this my wish for you.

CONCLUSION

All life force comes from Source; so, too, are we the temple for Source in this physical body.

As this life force moves through your body, with each breath that you take, choose to bathe yourself in love, in compassion, in empathy, in understanding, in wisdom, in acceptance, taking the time to ground these frequencies of higher consciousness into your body.

— ❧ —

Finding inner peace and solitude creates a ripple effect which affects personal (individual) change.

Finding inner peace and solitude creates a ripple effect which affects both community as well as global (collective) change.

— ❧ —

Life is not about what happens to us but about the meaning we give to what happens to us.

———— ✦ ————

When you *know* that you are one with All That Is …… you are truly contented.

When you *know* that you are complete, that you are whole …… you are truly contented.

When you *know* that you are equal to everyone, but superior to none …… you are truly contented.

When you *know* that you are peace, that you are joy …… you are truly contented.

When you *know* that you are present, mindful, aware and conscious …… you are truly contented.

When you are truly contented, stating the words I AM will be sufficient for you will already *know* that you are everyone and everything.

We create our lives through our own thought processes. What you say creates what you believe. What you believe impacts how you behave. What you believe impacts the choices you make. What you believe impacts the way your life will be. You are the legacy that you leave behind.

———

In the words of Dr. Amit Goswami, Theoretical Nuclear Physicist, University of Oregon Institute of Theoretical Science ... *If ordinary people really knew that consciousness, and not matter, is the link that connects us with each other and the world, then their views about war and peace, environmental pollution, social justice, religious values and all other human endeavors would change radically.*

———

To be yourself in a world that is constantly trying to make you something else is the greatest accomplishment.

Ralph Waldo Emerson

In the words of Steve Maraboli ... *When I accept myself, I am freed from the burden of needing you to accept me.*

Jim Morrison, of the Doors, was an amazing individual. These are his words.

The most important kind of freedom is to be what you really are. You trade in your reality for a role. You trade in your sense for an act. You give up your ability to feel, and, in exchange, put on a mask. There can't be any large scale revolution until there's a personal revolution, on an individual level. It's got to happen inside first.

Psalm 82:6 says ...... *I have said Ye are gods; and all of you are children of the most High.*

John 10:34 says ...... *Jesus answered them, Is it not written in your law, I said, Ye are Gods?*

It was Plotinus who said ...... *Thus in sum, the Soul, a divine being and a dweller in the loftier realms, has entered body: it is a god.* Author of <u>The Enneads</u>, Plotinus also stated that real happiness was dependent on the metaphysical and authentic human being.

In the words of Vernon Linwood Howard ...... *We can accept God becoming man to save man, but not man becoming God to save himself.*

———— ✍ ————

These are powerful words, are they not?

As individuated aspects of Source, can it not be said that we are all Gods?

As individuated aspects of Source, each human soul has the potential, the power, the ability, to emulate the lives of those who have come before us, courtesy of the Eightfold Path.

They came so that we, with eyes to see, would see.

They came so that we, with ears to hear, would hear.

Do not take everything that I have shared herein as being the sole ultimate truth.

It is imperative that you take the time to explore, and further discern, the truth for yourself by [1] becoming aware of your true essence and [2] tapping into your authentic power.

I am here to do naught but heal my soul by living a deeply empowered, spiritually aware, and authentic life.

A new spin on an old adage ......

Row, row, row your boat gently down the stream (of consciousness, of awakening, of wisdom, of intelligence, of compassion, of empathy, of love, of acceptance). *Merrily, merrily, merrily, life is but a dream.*

A dream wherein you can decide what happens, you can choose what you become, you can choose how you react.

The physical world changes in congruence with the shifting (altering) of your thoughts and emotions.

——— ೀ ———

Thank you for sharing this dream with me.

NAMASTE

Namaskār, also known as Namastē, is a form of greeting practiced most in the Indian Subcontinent. [24]

It is used both while greeting and upon parting company.

When a person greets another with Namaskār, the greeting is accompanied by a slight bow made with hands pressed together, palms touching and fingers pointed upwards and closely positioned in front of the chest.

Namaskār is pronounced like nah-mas-khar.

Namastē is pronounced like nah-mah-stay.

Along with this greeting, the words are also vocalized.

---

[24] http://www.spiritualresearchfoundation.org/spiritual-living/how-should-we-greet/namaskar-namaste-meaning/

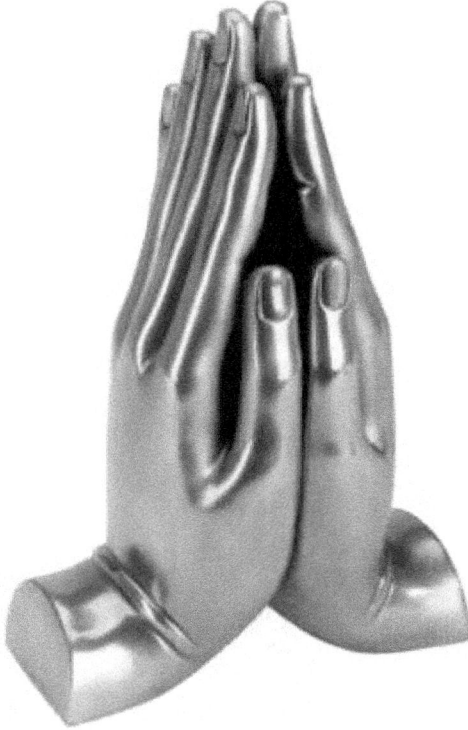

The hand position is known as the Namaskar Mudra (a mudra is a particular hand gesture or position).

Within each of us there exists the Divine (God Principle) known as the soul (*ātmā*); the greeting of Namaskār is when the Soul in one person acknowledges and pays reverence (homage, respect) to the Soul in another. [25]

With this greeting as there is no physical contact, but one does close their eyes, thereby facilitating the process for one to *see* within in order to focus on the soul (God) within the individual. [26]

---

[25] http://www.spiritualresearchfoundation.org/spiritual-living/how-should-we-greet/namaskar-namaste-meaning/
[26] Ibid.

CHAPTER BIBLIOGRAPHY

PERSONAL AFFIRMATIONS

Affirm Your Life [27]

Manifest Your Magnificence [28]

Positive Affirmations [29]

Positive Affirmations for Life Program [30]

Positive Affirmations: Money Series [31]

Positive Affirmations to Empower Yourself and Enhance Your Life [32]

---

[27] http://affirmyourlife.blogspot.com/
[28] http://www.amazon.com/Manifest-Magnificence-Affirmation-Cards-Years/dp/0973038004
[29] http://www.creatinginsight.co.uk/Beliefs-and-Behaviours/positive-affirmations.html
[30] https://www.prolificliving.com/affirmations/
[31] https://www.prolificliving.com/affirmations-money/
[32] http://www.robinskey.com/positive-affirmations-to-empower-yourself-and-enhance-your-life/

Powerful Money Affirmations [33]

Reconnecting with the Spirit of Money [34]

The Affirmation Spot [35]

The Only 100 Positive Affirmations You Will Ever Need [36]

Your Cells Are Listening: How Talking To Your Body Helps You Heal [37]

I AM

Documentary: I AM [38] [39]

---

[33] http://powerfulmoneyaffirmations.com/
[34] https://ascension101.com/en/estore/exercises/product/48-reconnecting-with-the-spirit-of-money.html
[35] http://www.theaffirmationspot.com/positive-thinking.html
[36] http://www.prolificliving.com/100-positive-affirmations/
[37] http://thespiritscience.net/2015/08/07/your-cells-are-listening-how-talking-to-your-body-helps-you-heal/
[38] http://www.iamthedoc.com/
[39] http://www.one.org/us/2011/04/05/review-documentary-i-am-emphasizes-the-power-of-one/

I AM [40]

I AM Infinite Power [41]

I AM THAT I AM: The First Breath [42]

Pastor Joel Osteen's Full Sermon entitled THE POWER OF I AM [43]

Self Love Affirmations [44]

Tapping Into Your True Potential: Unleashing The Power of I AM (hosted by Howard Falco) [45]

The Power of Affirmation and The I AM Factor [46]

---

[40] http://www.abundance-and-happiness.com/power-of-i-am.html
[41] http://thespiritofwater.com/pages/i-am-infinite-power
[42] http://powerofbreath.com/articles/i-am-that-i-am-the-first-breath/
[43] http://www.oprah.com/oprahs-lifeclass/Pastor-Joel-Osteens-Full-Sermon-on-The-Power-of-I-Am-Video_1
[44] http://iamuniversity.org/self-love-affirmations/
[45] http://www.synchcast.net/#!iam/c212r
[46]
http://elijahmitimotivation.webstarts.com/uploads/THE_I_AM_FACTOR.pdf

The Power of I AM [47] [48] [49] [50] [51] [52] [53]

The Power of I AM and The Law of Attraction [54]

The Power of I AM in Healing, Forgiving and Moving Through Difficult Situations [55]

The Power of I AM Statements [56]

The Power of I AM Vortex [57]

Why Oprah Says the Words I AM Matter [58]

---

[47] http://www.audioenlightenment.com/the-power-of-i-am
[48] http://www.dailyom.com/library/000/000/000000607.html
[49] http://ascension-research.org/i_am.html
[50] http://www.powerofiambook.com/
[51] https://www.linkedin.com/pulse/power-i-am-seth-r-
[52] http://karenklassen.ca/the-power-of-i-am/
[53] http://mariaerving.com/power-of-i-am/
[54] http://www.audible.com.au/pd/Health-Personal-Development/The-Power-of-I-AM-and-the-Law-of-Attraction-Audiobook/B00KDPD202
[55] http://www.naturalnews.com/046664_positive_thinking_mindful_meditation_healing.html
[56] http://mirellietc.com/the-power-of-i-am-statements/
[57] http://www.infinite-manifesting.org/IAMVortex.html
[58] http://www.oprah.com/oprahs-lifeclass/Why-Oprah-Says-the-Words-I-Am-Matter-Video_2

ABOUT THE AUTHOR

Michele Doucette is webmistress of Portals of Spirit, a spirituality website whereby one will find links to categories of interest from Angels to Zen, books of spiritual resonance, videos and documentaries. In addition, she holds a Crystal Healing Practitioner diploma (Stonebridge College in the UK) and is guardian to many from the mineral kingdom.

As a Level 2 Reiki Practitioner, she sends long distance Reiki to those who make the request, claiming only to be a channeler of the Universal Energy, thereby allowing the individual(s) in question to heal themselves.

She is the author of spiritual/metaphysical works; namely, [1] <u>The Ultimate Enlightenment For 2012: All We Need Is Ourselves</u>, a book that was nominated for the AllBooks Review Best Inspirational Book of 2011, [2] <u>Turn Off The TV: Turn On Your Mind</u>, [3] <u>Veracity At Its Best</u>, [4] <u>The Collective: Essays on Reality</u> (a composition of essays in relation to the Matrix),

[5] Sleepers Awaken: The Time Is Now To Consciously Create Your Own Reality, [6] Healing the Planet and Ourselves: How To Raise Your Vibration, [7] You Are Everything: Everything Is You, [8] The Awakening of Humanity: A Foremost Necessity, [9] The Cosmos of The Soul: A Spiritual Biography, [10] Getting Out Of Our Own Way: Love Is The Only Answer, [11] Living The Jedi Way, [12] Vicarius Christi: The Vicar of Christ, [13] A Metaphysics Primer: Changing From The Inside Out, [14] The Cosmos of The Soul II: Messages, [15] Living The ED Principles and [16] Mary Magdalene: A Personal Connection all of which have been published through St. Clair Publications.

In addition, she has written another volume that deals solely with crystals, aptly entitled The Wisdom of Crystals.

The author of A Travel in Time to Grand Pré, this is a visionary metaphysical novel that historically ties the descendants of Yeshua (Jesus) to modern day Nova Scotia.

As shared by a reviewer, <u>Veracity At Its Best</u> "constructs the context for the spiritual message" imparted in <u>A Travel in Time to Grand Pré</u>.

Against the backdrop of 1754 Acadie, this novel, an alchemical tale of time travel, romance and intrigue, from Henry Sinclair to the Merovingians, from the Cathari treasure at Montségur to the Knights Templar, also blends French Acadian history with current DNA testing.

Together with the words of Yeshua as spoken at the height of his ministry, <u>A Travel in Time to Grand Pré</u> has the potential to inspire others; for it is herein that we learn how individuals can find their way, their truth(s), so as to live their lives to the fullest.

Several years in the making, she was also driven to write <u>Back Home With Evangeline</u>, the sequel. It is here that Madeleine and Michel find themselves back in the twentieth century with a message that must be shared with the world. So, too, and even more importantly, must the message be lived, and experienced, by one and all.

She is also the author of <u>Time Will Tell</u>, a uniquely moving tale that begins in the present day before weaving its way backward through time to connect a glowing thread of historic discoveries.

Courtesy of past-life regression, Michaela (Dr. Mike) Callaghan, a brilliant metaphysical scientist, in the twenty-first century, discovers that she lived as a young, noble, Cathari herbalist healer, in the Languedoc area of France, during a time when political change was in the air.

The author of <u>Ad Infinitum: Unchanging and Forevermore</u>, a love story involving Ysabeau and Ghislain, twin souls who are successful in finding each other in the physical arena of the 21st century, this is a tome that delves into both incarnation (the process whereby the non-physical essence of Source is invested with physical form; a union of the physical plane of existence with the non-physical) as well as reincarnation (the re-cycling of this non-physical essence into different physical forms, different time periods and different roles, in order to experience all forms of materiality, to understand each thoroughly, and to learn how to manipulate, and maintain, these forms in balance and harmony); each is the sum total of past experiences, from various perspectives, over eons of existence.

When not working as a Special Education teacher, she continues to read, research and write, exploring her personal genealogies, all of which constitute her passion.

In the words of the Dalai Lama ... *In order to be happy, one must first possess inner contentment; and inner contentment cannot come from having all we want; rather it comes from having and appreciating all we have.*